11/13

P9-EMF-403

WOW!
SURPRISING FACTS ABOUT
I didn't know that
ANIMALS

Goats have rectangular pupils!

KINGFISHER
LONDON & NEW YORK

Copyright © Kingfisher 2013
Published in the United States by Kingfisher,
175 Fifth Ave., New York, NY 10010
Kingfisher is an imprint of Macmillan Children's Books, London.
All rights reserved.

Distributed in the U.S. and Canada by Macmillan, 175 Fifth Ave., New York, NY 10010

Library of Congress Cataloging-in-Publication data has been applied for.

Author: Emma Dods
Design and styling: Amy McSimpson
Jacket design: Mike Davis
Illustrations: Marc Aspinall
Consultant: John Woodward

ISBN: 978-0-7534-7117-3

Kingfisher books are available for special promotions and premiums.
For details contact: Special Markets Department, Macmillan, 175 Fifth Ave., New York, NY 10010.

For more information, please visit www.kingfisherbooks.com

Printed in China
1 3 5 7 9 8 6 4 2
1TR/0413/WKT/UG/140WFO

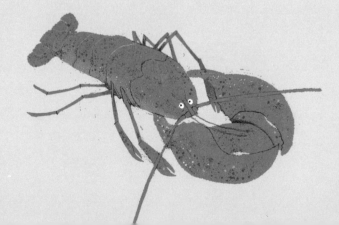

WOW!
I didn't know that
SURPRISING FACTS ABOUT ANIMALS

Gorillas never sleep in the same nest for more than one night.

A group of gorillas that live together is called a troop or band.

Gorillas can catch human colds!

KINGFISHER
NEW YORK

Some people think that an ostrich buries its head in the ground. From a distance, when an ostrich turns the eggs in its nest, its head disappears. This makes it look like it is buried, but it isn't really!

An ostrich is a bird, but it cannot fly! It can run at a speedy 45 miles (70km) per hour, though.

One ostrich egg weighs as much as 24 chicken's eggs. These huge eggs are around 6 inches (15cm) long and 5 inches (13cm) wide. It would take about an hour and a half to hard-boil one of them.

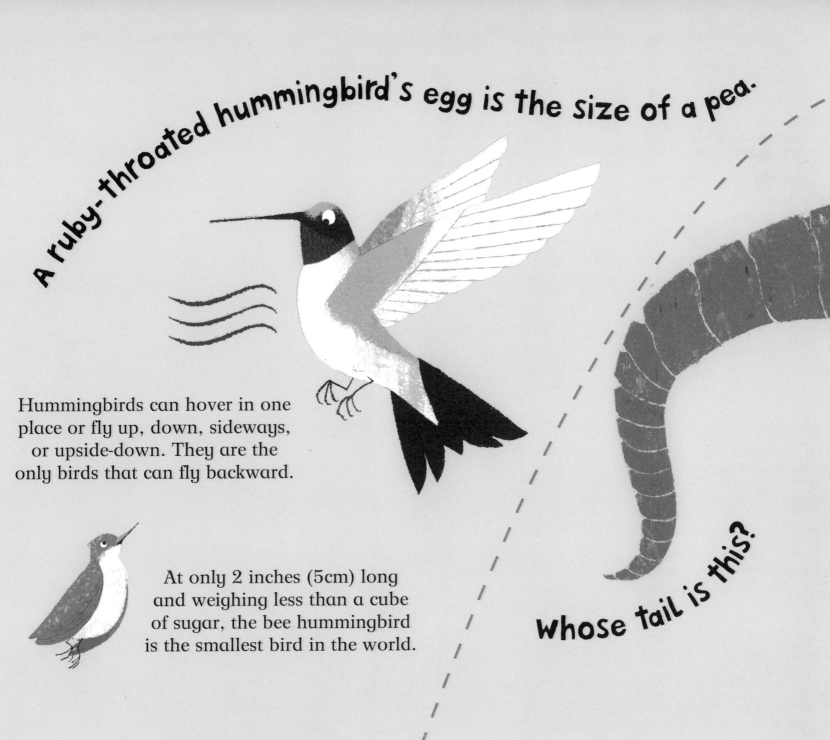

A ruby-throated hummingbird's egg is the size of a pea.

Hummingbirds can hover in one place or fly up, down, sideways, or upside-down. They are the only birds that can fly backward.

At only 2 inches (5cm) long and weighing less than a cube of sugar, the bee hummingbird is the smallest bird in the world.

whose tail is this?

After a hummingbird has gobbled up a fly, it only takes ten minutes for it to come out of the other end.

These fierce reptiles store fat in their tail and can survive for a long time without food—up to two years for some adults.

5

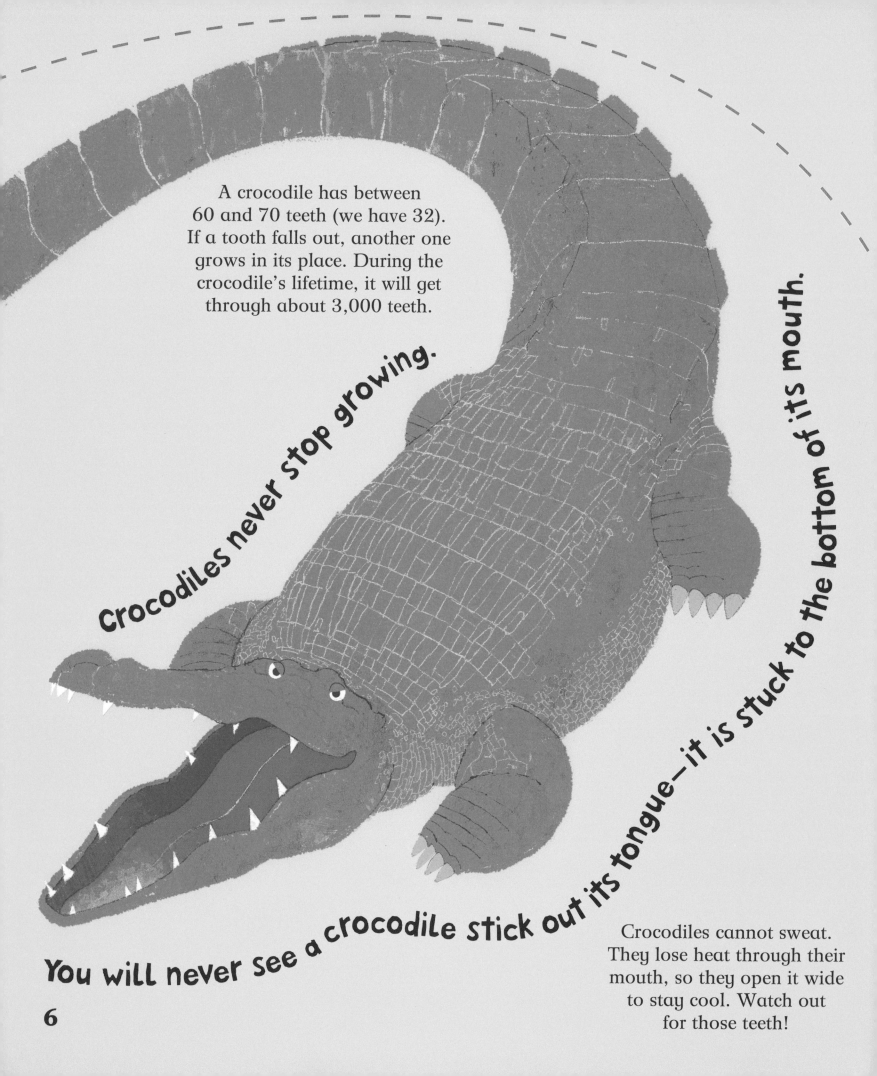

A crocodile has between 60 and 70 teeth (we have 32). If a tooth falls out, another one grows in its place. During the crocodile's lifetime, it will get through about 3,000 teeth.

Crocodiles never stop growing.

it is stuck to the bottom of its mouth.

You will never see a crocodile stick out its tongue—

Crocodiles cannot sweat. They lose heat through their mouth, so they open it wide to stay cool. Watch out for those teeth!

Cats can purr but not roar. Big cats, such as lions and tigers, can roar but not purr.

A lion's roar is so loud that it can be heard from more than 5 miles (8km) away.

roooarrr

A lion cannot roar until it is one year old.

purrrr

Some cats are right-pawed, and some are left-pawed.

Does a cheetah roar or purr? Go to page 19 to find out!

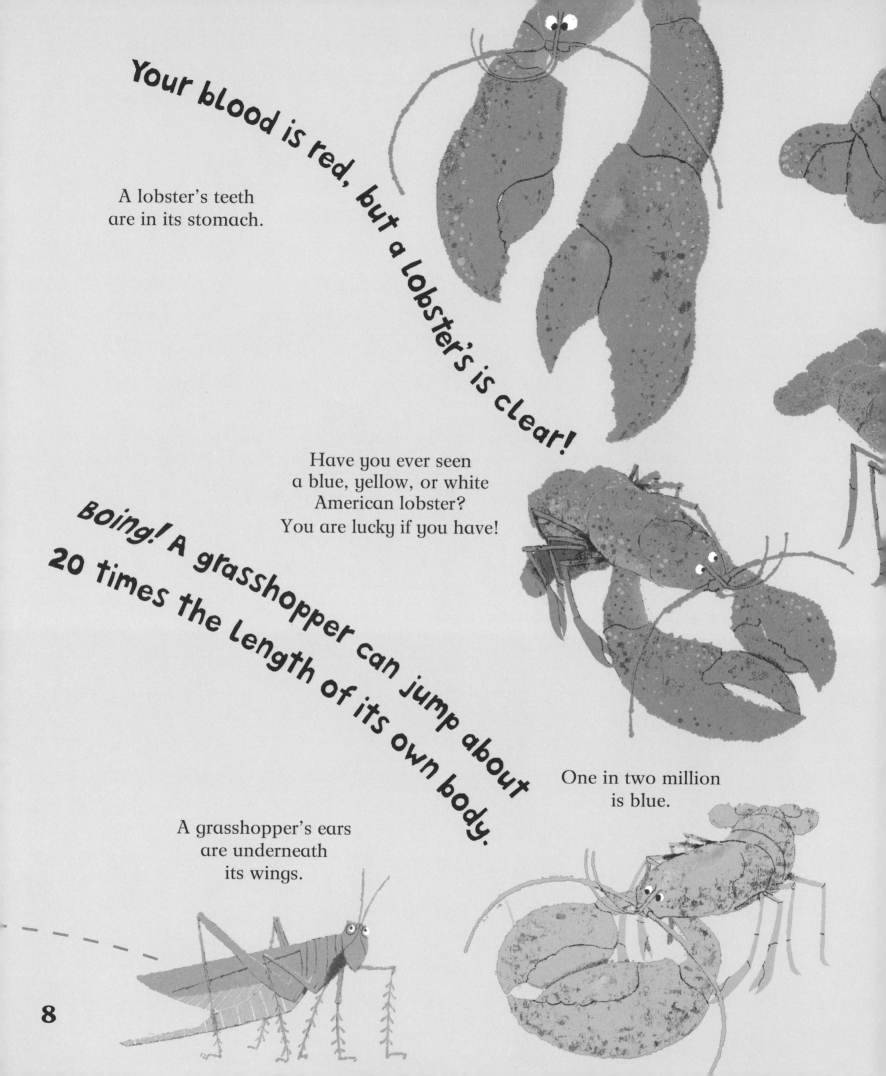

Your blood is red, but a Lobster's is clear!

A lobster's teeth are in its stomach.

Have you ever seen a blue, yellow, or white American lobster? You are lucky if you have!

Boing! A grasshopper can jump about 20 times the Length of its own body.

One in two million is blue.

A grasshopper's ears are underneath its wings.

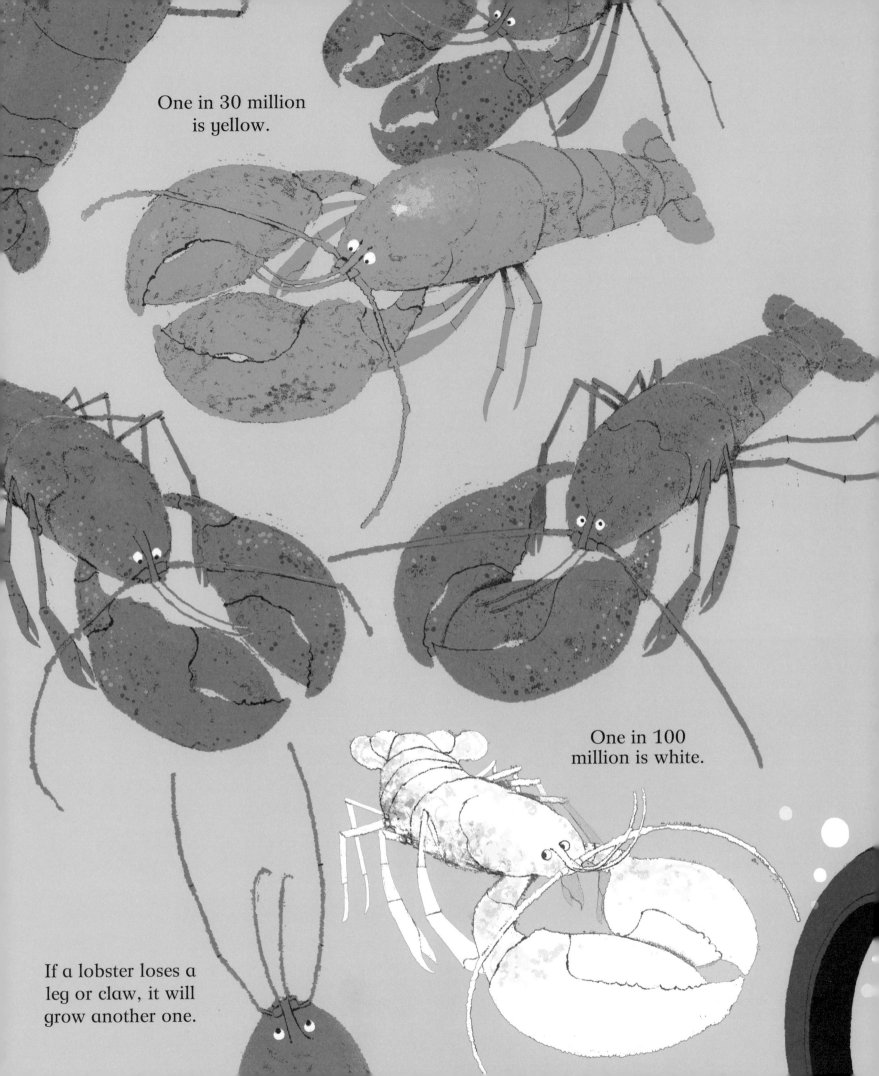

One in 30 million
is yellow.

One in 100
million is white.

If a lobster loses a
leg or claw, it will
grow another one.

Sharks don't have any bones. Their skeletons are made from a bendy material called cartilage— just like your ears are.

Sharks live in every ocean in the world.

There are about 370 types of sharks, but most aren't dangerous to humans. Tiger sharks like this one are, though!

Tiger sharks eat almost anything, from turtles and birds to fish and other sharks. They are even known to gobble up oil cans, tires, and car license plates. Yuck!

Flying fish escape from their enemies, such as sharks, by gliding through the air on winglike fins.

Flying fish can glide for more than 160 feet (50m)—around the length of two tennis courts.

The sperm whale has the largest brain in the world. It is 13 times bigger than an adult human's brain.

A sperm whale can hold its breath for up to 40 minutes at a time as it dives deep down into the ocean.

The blue whale is the biggest animal that has ever lived!

A blue whale can be up to 108 feet (33m) long— around the length of a basketball court.

Whales sing to each other underwater. These songs can travel for incredible distances—sometimes from one side of an ocean to the other.

12

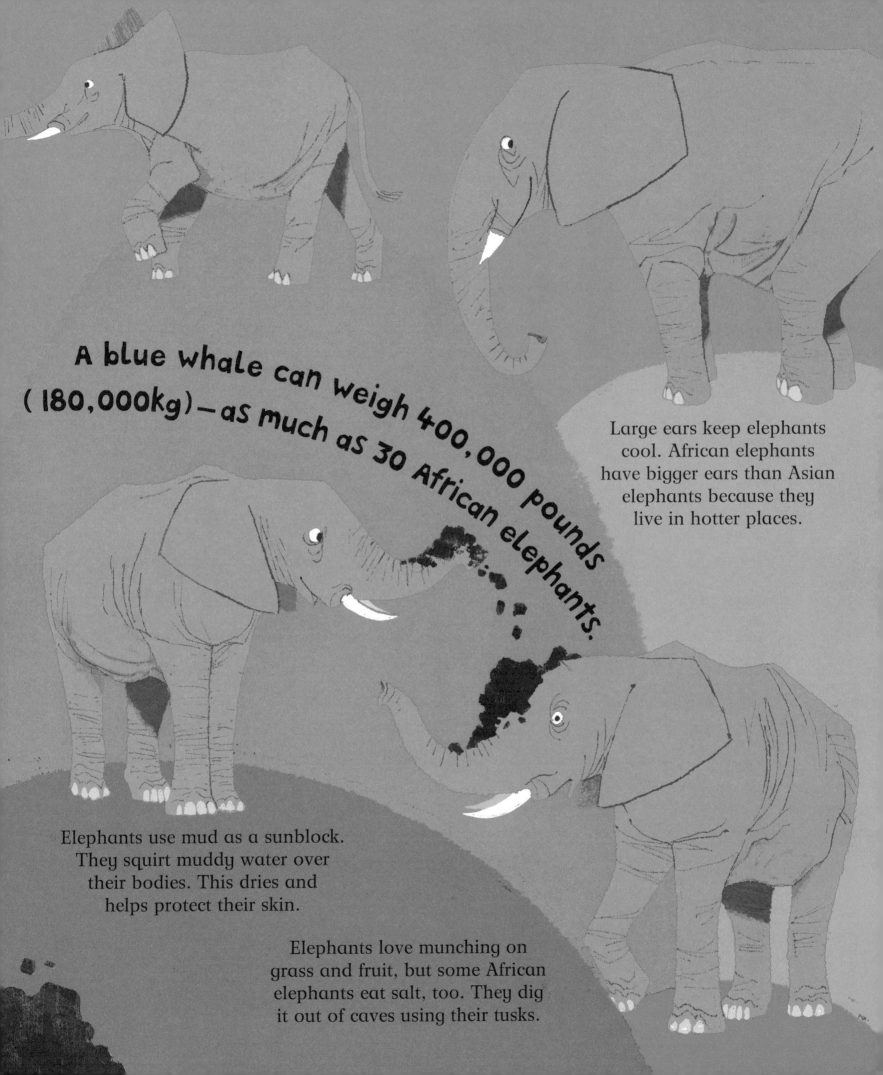

A blue whale can weigh 400,000 pounds (180,000kg)—as much as 30 African elephants.

Large ears keep elephants cool. African elephants have bigger ears than Asian elephants because they live in hotter places.

Elephants use mud as a sunblock. They squirt muddy water over their bodies. This dries and helps protect their skin.

Elephants love munching on grass and fruit, but some African elephants eat salt, too. They dig it out of caves using their tusks.

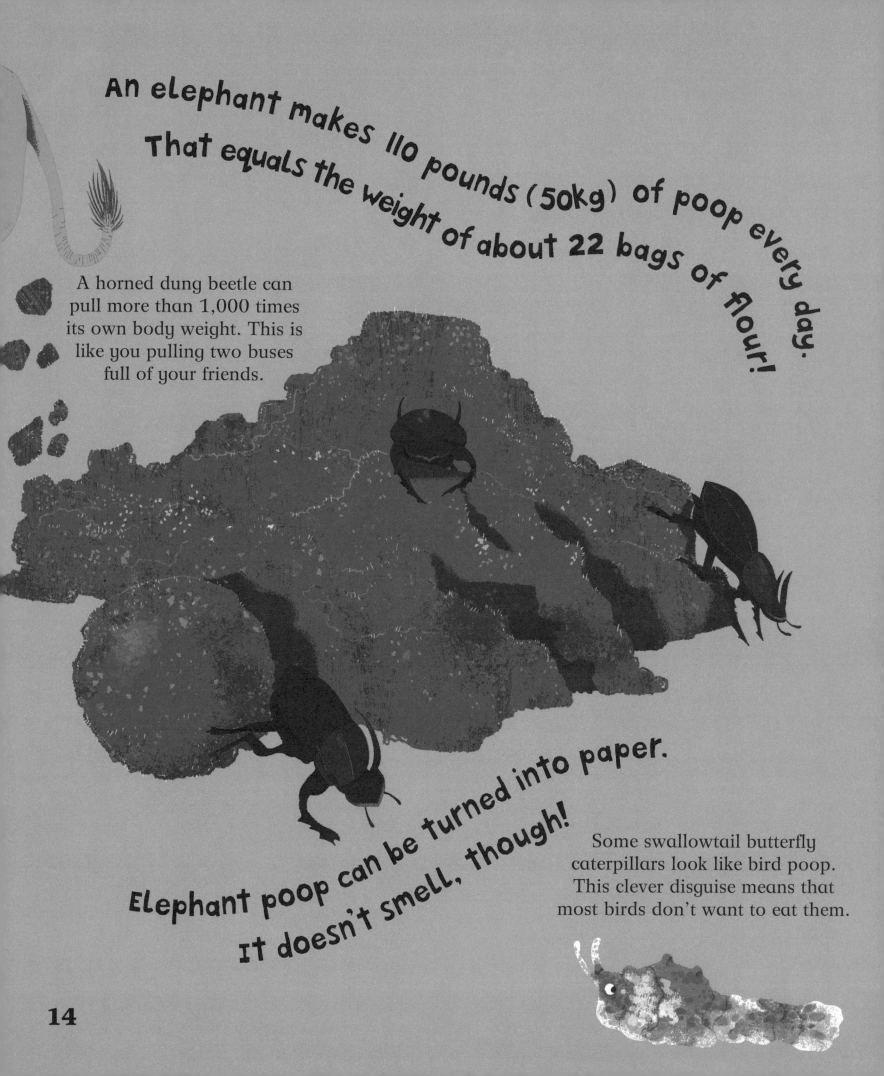

An elephant makes 110 pounds (50kg) of poop every day. That equals the weight of about 22 bags of flour!

A horned dung beetle can pull more than 1,000 times its own body weight. This is like you pulling two buses full of your friends.

Elephant poop can be turned into paper. It doesn't smell, though!

Some swallowtail butterfly caterpillars look like bird poop. This clever disguise means that most birds don't want to eat them.

The most expensive coffee in the world is made using coffee beans that Asian palm civets have eaten and then pooped out.

whose paw is this?

Civets perfume their poop with something called musk. Believe it or not, some of the most expensive perfumes contain civet musk.

Koalas have fingerprints that look just like ours. Even a police officer couldn't tell the difference.

When a koala is born, it looks like a pink jellybean.

Koalas sleep for about 19 hours each day.

16

Kangaroos cannot move backward.

BOING!

Koalas look like bears, but they actually belong to a group of animals called marsupials. Kangaroos are also marsupials.

Kangaroos are good swimmers. When they swim, they can move one foot at a time. On land, they can only move both feet together.

A mole can dig 100 feet (30m) of tunnels a day.

A mole can move backward through the tunnels and turn around by doing a somersault.

Follow the dotted line to discover the winner.

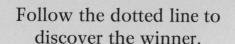

Hippos are heavy, but they are also speedy. They can reach speeds of up to 20 miles (30km) per hour.

Big dragonflies can zip along at 40 miles (60km) per hour. Not bad for such small animals!

cheetahs are the fastest animals on four legs. They can run at 71 miles (114km) per hour.

The fastest humans can sprint at 27 miles (44km) per hour.

The name "hippopotamus" comes from two greek words that mean "river horse."

A cheetah purrs— it cannot roar!

A cheetah can go from 0 to 60 miles (96km) per hour in less than three seconds—quicker than a racecar.

19

With its long neck, the giraffe is the tallest animal on Earth. Its eyes can be up to 20 feet (6m) off the ground, giving it an amazing view.

Giraffes have the same number of neck bones as us—they are just longer!

What sounds do giraffes make? They can moo, hiss, and even whistle!

The fastest animal of all is the peregrine falcon. It attacks its prey in a high-speed dive, zooming through the sky at up to 200 miles (320km) per hour.

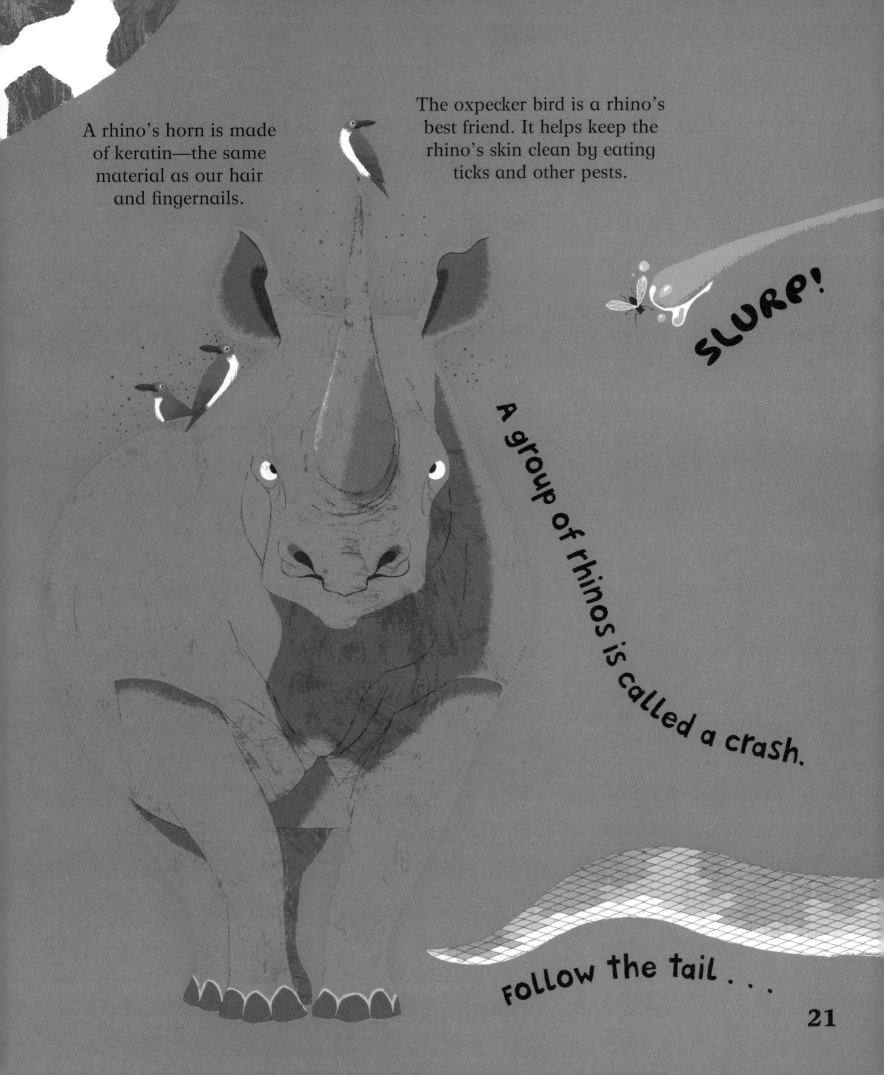

A rhino's horn is made of keratin—the same material as our hair and fingernails.

The oxpecker bird is a rhino's best friend. It helps keep the rhino's skin clean by eating ticks and other pests.

SLURP!

A group of rhinos is called a crash.

Follow the tail . . .

A chameleon has weird, scaly eyes that can look in two directions at the same time.

A chameleon's sticky tongue can be as long as its body, making it perfect for gobbling up tasty insects.

Chameleons can change color, depending on how they feel. Excited chameleons have bright patterns, but scared ones turn pale with fear!

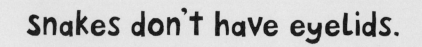

Snakes don't have eyelids.

The fastest spider on Earth is the European giant house spider. It can sprint across your carpet at just over 1 mile (2km) per hour.

The webs of giant golden silk orb-weaver spiders are so strong that fishermen and women in the south Pacific Ocean use them as fishnets!

A snake smells things by using its tongue! That's why it flicks its tongue in and out.

hisssssss

Monarch butterflies flutter across North America to find food.

The birdwing butterflies of New Guinea are as big as birds. Their wings are up to 12 inches (30cm) across. That's almost as wide as this book.

The glass frog is see-through!

CROAK!

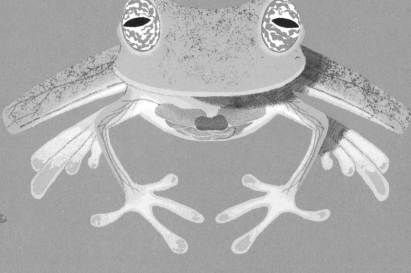

A group of frogs is called an army.

When a frog pushes its food down its throat, it uses muscles that are attached to the backs of its eyes. This makes its eyes pop in and out.

Sometimes, they even fly across the Atlantic Ocean.

Little bugs called aphids suck juice from plants and make a sweet liquid called honeydew. Ants love this, so they farm the aphids like we farm cows. The ants gather the aphids together and take care of them.

Army ants make a nest at night using their own bodies. They cling onto each other's feet to form a ball. This is to protect their queen and her young.

Flamingos are bright pink because of what they eat. The tiny living creatures that they munch on contain red chemicals. This makes their white feathers turn pink.

Flamingos eat with their head upside down to strain their food from the water.

Flamingos rest by standing on just one leg.

An owl's huge eyes are locked in its skull, so it cannot move them at all. It has to move its entire head to look in a different direction.

Most owls live in trees, but some live in burrows.

What a wing! A wandering albatross has an incredible wingspan. It can be 11.5 feet (3.5m) from the tip of one wing to the other.

The wandering albatross can fly for days without flapping its wings. It soars around Antarctica on ocean winds like a glider.

Dogs were some of the first animals to be sent into space.

Dogs can sweat only through their feet.

Dogs can be trained to detect explosives, drugs, and even diseases.

A flea can jump up to a height of 12 inches (30cm). That's the same as you jumping over a skyscraper!

The penguins on Zavodovski Island in the Antarctic have central heating. The island is an active volcano, and all the hot rock inside of it helps keep the penguins warm.

Female emperor penguins lay one egg each and then leave to go hunting. During the 17 weeks that they are away, each male penguin takes care of an egg. The males don't have anything to eat while they wait!

Emperor penguins are the only birds that lay their eggs on ice. To stop the eggs from freezing, they rest them on their feet.

Polar bears can swim nonstop for hundreds of miles.

A polar bear can eat 88 pounds (40kg) of meat at a time—that's probably roughly what you weigh . . .

Polar bears usually get too hot rather than too cold!

Polar bears have black skin and clear hairs. The hairs are not white—they just appear to be.

If an octopus loses one of its eight arms, it can grow another one!

octopuses cannot hear.

octopuses have blue blood.

Sea anemones are the perfect hiding place for anemone fish, or clownfish. They are the only fish that don't get stung by the anemone's tentacles.

All anemone fish are born male. Some then change into females.

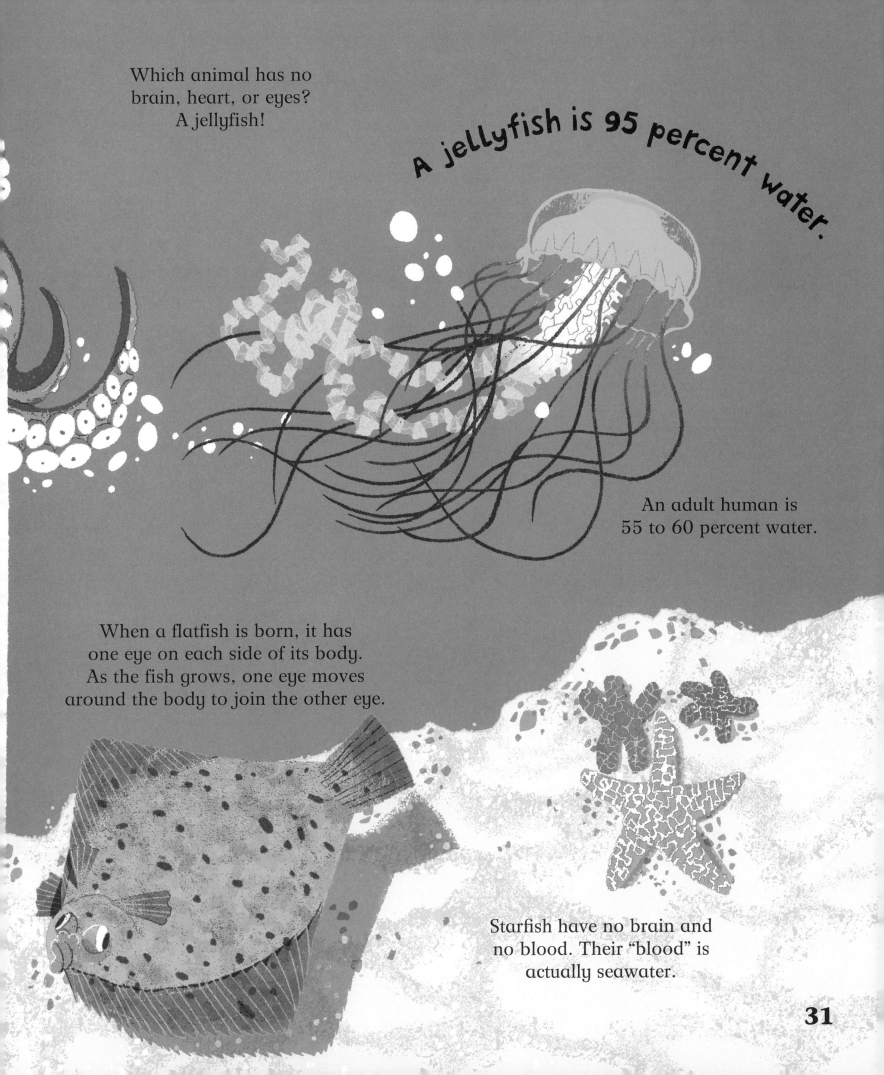

Which animal has no brain, heart, or eyes? A jellyfish!

A jellyfish is 95 percent water.

An adult human is 55 to 60 percent water.

When a flatfish is born, it has one eye on each side of its body. As the fish grows, one eye moves around the body to join the other eye.

Starfish have no brain and no blood. Their "blood" is actually seawater.

31

A woodpecker's tongue is so long that it wraps around the back of its skull. The tongue scoops out insects from holes in trees.

Each tiger has its own pattern of stripes on its fur. No two tigers are the same.

A tiger's skin is striped, as well as its fur!

Prairie dogs are North American ground squirrels that live together in big networks of burrows. Some of these prairie dog towns can be as large as human cities!